Sprig of Lilac
A Poetry Collection

by Kelsey Bigelow

Copyright © 2018 Kelsey Bigelow.

All rights reserved. This book or any portion thereof may not be reproduced or used in any manner whatsoever without the express written permission of the publisher except for the use of brief quotations in a book review.

Cover photo by Katie Daley.

Cover and book design by Terry Followell.

Published in the United States by CreateSpace, an Amazon Company.

First edition, 2018.

kelkaybpoetry.com
facebook.com/kelkaybpoetry
instagram.com/kelkayb

For the grievers

THE CONTENTS

INTRODUCTION	1
Mourning Is Melancholia	2
I envy you	3
A Conversation	4
Eyelash Noises	5
Hi	6
With Ever Returning Mourn	7
How To Live On	9
Things Death Teaches You	11
November 16, 2014	12
How Many Lives?	13
How am i supposed to say it	15
Cardinal Dysfunction	16
Retrospection :	
Understanding Brought By Grief	17
May 3, 1971	18
Hold True	20
Soul Records For The Soul Wrecker	23
A Little Late Motherly Advice	24
Today I Choose A Life	26
May 3, 2018	27
A Motherless Daughter	28
November 16, 2016	29
WORKS CITED	31
ACKNOWLEDGEMENTS	32

INTRODUCTION

What lies ahead is the embodiment of an individual's grieving process. No two people grieve in the same order, time period, or severity; this work knows that. It does not try to explain why grief happens the way it does. This work simply wants to be the understanding ear that not every griever is lucky enough to have.

There are moments of text throughout this collection that come from other authors — all of whom receive credit in the works cited at the end and own the rights to their respective lines — combined with the poet's own lyric.

What lies ahead is not to be assumed as the true events of any real-life person. Any situational coincidences are strictly that, coincidences.

"Dreams serve us narcissistic light. We begin making conclusions. Melancholia fluctuates with certainty and suggests affection. Our impressions are indisputable. We drop validity and console ourselves with anything typical.

Mourning is melancholia.

Mourning involves departure from life, a reaction to the pain, loss of interest in the world because the loved no longer exists."

— Sigmund Freud (sort of)

I ENVY YOU

You who didn't have to
go about your day
for 3,245 days
lying to anyone
who asks if you're okay
while being consumed
with unrealistic dreams
of having your mom
at your college graduation

You did not have
to sit helpless
as she seized
for the third time
in two days
for the fourth weekend
in a row or
have to help her feel normal
while being aware that
your hand over hers
was exponentially stronger
and the thought of hugging her
meant holding her into dust
You did not have
to live your life
while hers was slowly ending

But you do have to
live your life without her
and for that
I feel you

A Conversation

They take you off the resuscitator
Your body mimicks the pumping

I slide the hair
from your forehead
and whisper
I love you

                                You lift your index finger
                                      on the hand
                                      closest to me

I kiss your forehead
and whisper
I'm going to miss you

                                          A tear falls from
                                            your left eye

                and gently you pass into
                          eversleep

Eyelash Noises
Co-Written By Tony Lieb

The silence had grown violent
to the point of hearing air between eyelashes
as I blinked the salt down my cheek

and even though her hands had grown cold
she wiped my eyes as I said goodbye
Then she gave me her eyes for a second of time
before she faded to white

Hi,

When our girl called
saying you passed,
I felt like an ass
for everything that happened:
the custody battle we put them
through, the compromise I refused,
the money we fought over
they never paid attention to,
even the lies about being
"just friends" with *her*.
As I look at this dumb apple-shaped
salt shaker that you threw
at my shoulder,
it all seems pointless.
And even though I could never say it
out loud, watching our girl load the bowls
on the top shelf of the dishwasher
makes me happy that she has
more of you in her than me.
I glance at the save-the-date
for our oldest, held up
by your *Sound of Music* magnet
and can't help but think
~~they should have you at their weddings.~~
~~I shouldn't become a grandparent without you.~~
~~I haven't even lost my own mother yet.~~
they shouldn't have to experience this before me.

With Ever-Returning Mourn

                                        My hardest funeral was a woman
                  who saw light in everyone and lived with no regrets.
                                There was a stream of faces
                                that were so sorry for our distress.
                        Don Williams sang in the background
                                    as we three kids held hands.

Oh, how shall I warble myself
for the dead one there I loved?

                              I wanted to sing with her once more,
                                  so I quietly sang with Don.
                            I remember my brothers joining in.

And how shall I deck my song
for the large sweet soul that has gone?

                                  The night before our hardest day,
                                      I laughed with Grandma
                          as we messed up our Triominoes game.

                                                We cried, too.

I mourn'd, and yet shall mourn
with ever-returning fall.

                        That morning, it was as if Mom was saying,
                              "Smile baby girl, it's sunrise."

                  That day, I watched as Grandpa sat on the floor and
                                  said repeatedly to his cat,
                          "I love you, Babe. I love you, Babe."
                 I realized that was how he was going to grieve.

Here, coffin that slowly passes,
I give you my sprig of lilac.

                                        "So the separated husband
                               and the ex-husband go to the funeral…"
                      I realized that was how Dad was going to grieve,
                            so I laughed at his awkwardly timed joke.

                                                                    I cried, too.

                              I remember praying I could someday
                                   be everything she hoped I would.

                                               I remember crying, too.

How To Live On

Let your body freeze
as you bury your mother
The woman who used to regularly
miss phone calls while driving
because her music was about
five notches louder
than any normal person
would have considered loud

Don't
leave the graveside
That means she's no longer
part of the world that she spent
too much time trying to improve
one stray kitten at a time
and one unsolicited yet genuine smile
at a time because
she never met a stranger

Don't
realize your legs
unthaw and carry you
back to the synthetic world
back to work and to people
who have yet to be scathed
to people who tilt their heads
and scrunch their eyebrows
as you pass by them

Become numb to their unknowing sympathy
and wait for them to forget
so you can continue to remember

Things Death Teaches You
Co-Written By Tony Lieb

    Tragedy makes that ambulance in the distance uncomfortably close

Waking up to crying and beeping
is better than closing my eyes
to beeping and weeping

                Time is different on the clocks of hospitals

At the receiving line
there will be too many hands to shake and words to say
Some of the hands will be a finger short and
words will be spoken by the hands who have had too many

Sometimes trying to figure out what to do after
is as hard as getting through

         It's strange when you say you can't relate to anyone
            yet many people feel the same

You'll rather be around people that don't smile when they meet you
    but are there when you need them

           What we will do in the name of comfort is vulgar
                the difference is a smile

Of all the sounds
God chose voices
to fill heaven

November 16, 2014

On the drive to
your funeral the sun peered
under my visor and I asked,
what good is day
when you can't enjoy it?
You sent a flock
of sparrows to
surround my car.

But tonight,
The cityscape eliminates
iced cornfields that meet bare
trees branching into a perfect twilight.
I want to ask you,
what good is night, if I can't
see Cygnus or the dippers?

After they lowered you,
I avoided lunch and walked
the dirt road. Squinting, I asked
what good is the sky if I
can't see into heaven? The face
of my angel only to be seen in pictures
of me in a crib or in a tasseled cap,
but not dressed in lace and ivory.
Now you form your new self
out of fading clouds.

Tonight, I go to bed dreaming of your
angel shape and ask
what good are clouds
if they take
the only light I had in my life?

HOW MANY LIVES?

Ten, I believe.

Five.

Not many, I'll say four. Well, maybe it was six. I know I was at more, but I can't remember. Ten. I've been to ten funerals.

                                              With my eight, that's thirty-three.

I think my maternal Grandfather's funeral was the hardest even though it was twenty-seven years ago. He was the first family member I remember dying.

Probably mother and father's.

                            How one can be more difficult to endure, I don't know.

A family friend's was probably hardest for me. Also my mom's. Mostly because I knew them better.

                            How do the living become altered when the dead depart?

                  We console ourselves with anything typical,
                      as we remember their gestures.

I feel like holding those still living even closer and often reevaluate my own life goals.

Some things just aren't as important and some things are even more important.

Life became more reflective.

I wish I could've spent more time with them.

                Time. Something I wish I had spent more of with my own mother.

I'm scared to suffer another loss knowing how heartbreaking it is to be drowned by grief's cruel hands that hold me powerless.

I realize there will be more funerals in the future and wonder how I will work through the emotions again.

                            How have I worked through my own emotions?

My mom's funeral was hard honestly because I had to watch my sisters suffer. There's no worse feeling than that.

I lost interest in the world.

My heart is there for family in our distress, but a couple of weeks later is when it hits me, and I get emotional.

                          As if burying a once living body isn't hard enough.

How am I supposed to say it
Co-Written By Tony Lieb

      when people finally let me say whatever I want
How I am to explain that
     at some point when we were all sitting there grieving
     my anger at him out drinking
         turned to pity
Pity for a man so clobbered
     he hides in a scotch glass
for a man so close to poor
     it looks more like hurt than dirt
     who spent his youth searching for cool
         and the rest looking for warmth
for a man we feared
     would hunt his demons
     so we took the gun from his apartment
a man who can't see that the world around him
     is not glamorous but meaningful
a man who believes smiles are worth something
     because people keep trying to steal his

Cardinal Dysfunction

Delinquent son, parenting from a cell
four hundred miles south of where
they buried his only motivator, will
never realize he can be better even
without her presence.

Distant father, a hundred
miles east of his first love's
grave, is busy with new kids
unable to relate to his oldest three.
Supporting them seems impossible
without their reason for living.

Stoic son in South Korea
marrying a woman the family
never met, plans to start a life a
thousand miles west, and avoids
those who still grieve
his over-protector.

Suppressed daughter,
two hundred miles north,
marks the skin between her key and
wrist, releasing anger and dwelling on
the absence of her first confidant.

Retrospection : Understanding Brought By Grief

her faith in us	:	belief that three good things existed in the world
saying our names	:	vocalization of "I love you"
her laugh	:	fake joy
her off-key singing	:	masked internal screams
polka dancing together	:	momentary mental escape
her cooking	:	an obligatory duty
her unsolicited advice	:	a wish to redo life
her love for animals	:	filling the void that grown children bring
her lack of height	:	being overlooked by everyone and everything
her long-distance support	:	an attempt at filling a home
her apple decorations	:	an attempt at filling a home
her hospitality	:	an attempt at filling a home
her heart of gold	:	the only proof of living
her snoring	:	exhaustion from living
her never-failing smile	:	contentment in agony
her hope she had for us	:	belief that something good would be left behind

May 3, 1971

Twenty-two years before you gave me life, you
began yours in a town of three hundred as

Pleasant Grove Memorial gained a headstone each year
that you were able to blow out another candle.

Visiting now, I see blacktop the town saved up for is pot-holed,
and the high school where you cartwheeled your way to

valedictorian has been torn down. It's just as you said,
nothing from this town lasts. Visiting now,

I understand how this town confined potential
and teenagers created lives to settle for.

You would've been forty-five today
but nothing from this town lasts. Even you

wound up returning as another headstone.

Hold True

Two years
of hearing the talkers talking and
now I know how to handle it in myself
      how to attend to it in others

I hear the talk of the beginning and the end
and am willing to not have any answers
but not to talk of the beginning or the end
      There was neither light nor heat

I do not talk of reality because I tire
of the incomprehension
and the dozens of proofs they invent
      She is everything that surrounds us
      that exists outside our consciousness
That cannot satisfy
      Two years
      Instead I talk of tiny things
I talk of her songs
      ignoring her four fingers of gin

and how she'd teach me to sing along
I talk of how we polkaed together for two hours
without speaking and how
we would bake pumpkin rolls without a sound

      You see
      words were often unnecessary
      since her current state had been full
      of undiscussed bruises

But I don't talk of the beginning or the end

        I talk of little things

like when she called to wish me luck at the prom
        despite the hundred and seventeen mile distance
or when she traveled to see me graduate
        clearly ignoring doctors' orders

or when she met my high school sweetheart
        and cried when she drank rum because
        she was loveless and fell short of not caring

But I do not talk of the beginning or the end

Instead I talk of normal things

I talk of the three
yes three
scrapbooks she crafted in a year's time
        as her motion began to cease

I talk of the text conversations when she gave
advice on my love life
        though she never quite got it right herself
I talk of the pride her eyes held when
her sixteen-year-old was going to bed
at ten o'clock on a Friday
        knowing she'd be up for another four hours
        because she was only two tequila shots in

        Two
            years

I do not talk of the end
because I didn't help
the middle or beginning

        Even with sober thoughts and a clear mind
        she had every right to fall to the bottom
        like an ice cube of an old fashioned

I do not talk of the beginning   middle   or end
       to shield the memories Grandma still holds
            allowing those to be the new truth

Though the talkers are talking of
an idealized version of the end
there is still the awful realization that
all laws of matter must hold true

            But I do not talk of the end

Soul Records For The Soul Wrecker
Co-Written By Tony Lieb

There is music you can escape to
Though I prefer music I can relate to
as it sometimes tightens my stomach
but eases my mind
You see
my soul rests in restlessness
It's not supposed to be this way
I pray for peace
But I'm afraid I have received it
and passed it along because it felt too light
to be worth anything

A Little Late Motherly Advice

You used to tell me how men refused to be constant
        like the two who gave you their word and a ring
            and you believed them
What you should have told me is that
the more men I meet
        the further they would be from knowing
        how you would hide in the bedroom
        press play on your Walkman
        and sing Lord I Hope This Day Is Good
        as if we couldn't hear you

You used to tell me to celebrate every birthday
like it was my first and last
        with poke-n-pour cake mixed in a bowl
        with three scoops of vanilla ice cream
What you should have told me is that
with each year that passes
        a new man waltzes over my brick that lies in a heap
        because you didn't teach me to stack it
        and finds your single dimple engraved in my smile
            which only appears
            when I hear your cackle in my mind

The last man endured my ache first hand
but the next will only be able to read my memories
He won't know
        the way your voice jumped two octaves
            when you were shocked
or the way you drank Capri Sun like it was water
He will have to take me at my word
        because all he sees is "Mother" engraved in marble

Today I Choose A Life

of unconditional certainty dressed
in a veil designed from your ivory. I walk

toward my groom without you there and think of how
you dressed in a gown altered to make room for your son

and walked toward the groom who revised your plans.
I can't help but wonder how you endured

your divorce and still had faith in the heart of another.
You said you didn't understand how God could have given you a

man capable of infidelity, who deemed
you unworthy. Yet you accepted

motherhood and rode away selfless.
Your second husband proved worse

with his spiteful love, which he shared
with more than just you. Yet

you remained faithful to both men in their times.
You would tell me

that they showed their love differently than others. You said
you did not need a gentler love, but wished one

for me. And, I know if you were here, you'd see that
the man at the end of the aisle will hold on and grow with me. You

would see that the man the end of the aisle will only ever touch me
with tenderness because you showed me what to look for,

so that I can ride away regretless.

May 3, 2018

I've seen your once-new divinity
in flocks and loose feathers
as you embodied mile markers
with each new road I came to

But

I've been feeling you around less

It's as if your final feathers
are holding on until my path illuminates
with moments
I may need motherly advice

Today though

Today I feel you a little heavier
Today you would've been 47

But there will be no
blown candles
sung songs
or birthday prayers

just absent flames
and airless hums
with my thumb
hovering over your old phone number
knowing the only voicemail I can leave
rests on the stem of a feather
with the hope of re-ascending

A Motherless Daughter

is a breed aside from the norm
She aches with a stillness turned tremor
mid aisle of the grocery or sanctuary
Some nights she weeps silent and alone
for the empty seat she knows will be listening to her vows
She regrows her shield
with the force of the shower on her neck
And though her pen etches into her core
sometimes that's her biggest solace

November 16, 2016

The hardest part is not
accepting I'll never hear you call me "Baby Girl" again
or hear you laugh when I'm unexpectedly sassy

It isn't
seeing the ballerina wall-hangings,
you bought me when I was four
or looking at the picture of us dressed in all leather
for my seventh birthday
not even holding the scrunchy you were wearing
that last day we spoke

The hardest part isn't
knowing you don't need me to re-microwave your coffee
again
It's not
the fact that you'll never watch
Simply Irresistible with me again
or sing along to "Wide Open Spaces"
for the hundred-and-first time

It is not
seeing your can of pumpkin filling
collect dust on the top shelf
or your pasta salad recipe
never quite tasting the same

It isn't
knowing you will never meet the woman I am becoming
or know the things I have accomplished

It isn't even
receiving pictures from Grandma of
your headstone surrounded by patches of dirt

The hardest part
is watching your grass grow

WORKS CITED

Abarca, Justin. "An Ode To Alcohol (When You Can No Longer Drink It)." BuzzFeed.com. 2016.

    "Hold True" contains lines from this article published on BuzzFeed.com.

Alleyne, Lauren. "Talking to the Dead." Difficult Fruit.

    "Hold True" contains lines from Lauren Alleyne's "Talking to the Dead."

Bentley, Alexander. "Eversleep: The Beauty of Dark Silence." Sosii Press, 1st edition. August 2017.

    "A Conversation" and "How To Live On" both include lines from Alexander Bentley's poetry collection Eversleep.

Bigelow, Kelsey. "May 3, 1971." Wisconsin's Best Emerging Poets: An Anthology, edited by Z Publishing House, 2017, pp. 86.

Freud, Sigmund. "Mourning and Melancholia." Collected Papers, Vol. IV. 152—170.

    The quotation introduction to "Sprig of Lilac" is an erasure of Sigmund Freud's "Mourning and Melancholia" essay, which is in the public domain.

"Hi" and "How Many Lives?" both include direct quotations from personal interviews with friends and family of the poet.

Whitman, Walt. Leaves of Grass. 1855.

    "With Ever-Returning Mourn" and "Hold True" include lines from Walt Whitman's Leaves of Grass, which is in the public domain.

ACKNOWLEDGEMENTS

These people are the reasons this collection exists:

- Dr. Kara Candito. My professor and mentor. Without you, I would not have had the motivation or confidence to write a single word during my most difficult times.
- The Cool Kids Crew. The workshop group that never failed to be brutally honest after I handed them a piece of my soul. Thank you for tearing each of these pieces apart to help me grow and discover what stories I was attempting to tell.
- Stephanie Walrack. My person. If it weren't for you, I probably would have bruised my head from hitting it on the side of my dorm bed. Thank you for always willingly reading my work even when you just wanted to be asleep. Love you, Stephie.
- Ashton Jordan. The writing friend I didn't know I was missing from my life. Thank you for reading, rereading, and re-rereading pieces that probably could've been complete five rounds of revisions ago. Thank you for pushing me through the times I doubted my abilities. I love you and am grateful for your friendship.
- Tony Lieb and Terry Followell, two of my favorite coworkers. Thank you to Tony for giving me the building blocks of the pieces we cowrote; your words brought more dimension to what I've been trying to portray, and I'm grateful. Thank you to Terry for voluntarily designing this collection, bringing my ink to life, and never failing to make my day.

» Every family member that read my poetry when it was still in its infant stages. Thank you for pretending the earlier versions of these pieces weren't lacking substance. Your support kept me pushing on.

» My angel momma. Though you're gone, you live and breathe within these pages. Your life inspires me every day to live as I am and to be better than I am. Losing you was indescribably awful, but it also was your final push for me to finally write like you always wanted. This is because of you and for you.

Made in the USA
Monee, IL
07 March 2023